CONTENTS

INTRODUCTION 5

Author's note

The first edition of the Time Management Pocketbook was written in 1990. Since then it has been bought by people all over the world who have been attracted to its practical straightforward approach to managing time.

However, in 1990 most of us didn't have mobile phones or laptop computers and email was in its infancy. We could safely leave our work and have a life outside without fear of being interrupted. The world has changed a lot since then.

We now demand that individuals be flexible and organisations respond to the needs of their customers. This has meant that we need to take a fresh look at the skills required to manage ourselves and see how they apply to this changing world.

I still believe that effective use of time calls for skills in a number of areas (see the model opposite). The help that you need depends on how you view time and on what skills you have. Remember that skills and techniques by themselves will not make you better, unless you incorporate them into a system or method that *works for you*.

Acknowledgements

To Martin Terry for the original concept and to Dr David Worth for his support, both formerly of Lucas Industries Group Training.

T.

THE TIME MANAGEMENT POCKETBOOK

6th Edition

By Ian Fleming

Drawings by Phil Hailstone

"This splendid little book respects our intelligence and time. It also puts to shame all the gimmicks to which we have been subjected of late."
Abdulla Ali Uqba, Chief Executive, Al Atheer, Development & Management Consultancy, Dubai

"More than just a guide to better managing your time - it's a collection of simple, yet effective, tips and reminders to help keep you on track."
Linda Harlow, Director, Brook Street plc

"Contains a wealth of practical tips to help busy managers manage their time better."
Viv Clements, Training Officer, Aylesbury Vale District Council

Published by:
Management Pocketbooks Ltd
Laurel House, Station Approach, Alresford, Hampshire SO24 9JH, U.K.
Tel: +44 (0)1962 735573 Fax: +44 (0)1962 733637
Email: sales@pocketbook.co.uk
Web: www.pocketbook.co.uk

© Ian Fleming 1990, 2003, 2011

1st edition 1990. Previous edition 2003 ISBN 978 1 903776 08 7
This edition 2011 ISBN 978 1 906610 37 1 Reprinted 2013

E-book ISBN 978 1 908284 00 6

British Library Cataloguing-in-Publication Data – A catalogue record for this book is available from the British Library.

Design, typesetting and graphics by **efex Ltd**. Printed in U.K.

THE MODEL

Managing what you do

Managing every day

Managing where you work

Managing to work with others

Managing communications

THE PRESSURES ON OUR TIME

Each day we are given 24 hours to live our lives – 86,400 seconds to spend. Many of us feel the need to cram as much as possible into each and every hour, both at work and in our leisure time.

It is possible to be in touch and on call virtually 24 hours a day. Information of all sorts is readily available wherever we are, on a bewildering variety of mobile devices, so we are fooled into thinking that it is both possible and necessary to see everything, read everything, know everything.

People are less able than ever to leave work behind, even on holidays. Social networking provides another pressure if you want to keep up, on a minute by minute basis, with everything in your friends' lives. When can you switch off?

The reality is that working all the time doesn't guarantee success, can cause unwanted stress and can make us vulnerable to accidents.

We have to make choices about what is important.

INTRODUCTION

THE PRESSURES ON OUR TIME

If technology was meant to make things easier, why does it feel as if there is more to do and less time to do it in than ever before?

- Businesses everywhere strive to achieve the maximum from the minimum, so people are put under great pressure to work at peak capacity all the time
- Timeframes have changed – everyone expects things to happen instantly, regardless of their relative importance
- Distractions are everywhere – it becomes harder to separate what is genuinely important from all that is shouting for your attention

It simply isn't possible to do everything, no matter how efficient your approach to managing time. You have to know what matters to you and where your priorities lie.

WHY IS TIME AN ISSUE FOR YOU?

Whatever your age and circumstances, you will have a particular reason for picking up this book.

For example, you:

- Have too much to do and are finding it hard to cope
- Want a better balance between work and leisure
- Are highly skilled and want some help achieving your goals
- Find yourself having to deal with people whose lack of time management makes your job harder
- Are entering the job market and need to be more organised
- Realise that your current approach to time is not working and you need to try something different

The person who can master their time can master nearly everything

INTRODUCTION

WHERE TO START

As a starting point, stand back and ask yourself what you want from your life.

What's important to you: your work, time with your family, making a contribution to society by helping others or simply enjoying yourself?

Understanding what is important will give you a focus for:
- How you want to spend your time
- Any help that you are looking for and, more importantly ...
- A reason to start taking **control** over your time

To get the most out of this book, don't simply look to collect techniques but decide if they would be of any help. If so, remember that you still need the discipline to apply them.

To manage your time better you've got to start to manage yourself.

WHAT COULD STOP YOU?

LINKING EFFORT TO BENEFITS

Most of what is contained in this book is common sense - but, alas, not always common practice. Why is this?

One explanation is that our behaviour is often guided by the amount of pleasure we gain from doing something.

For example, we enjoy being driven by events, crises, fire-fighting. Sound time management techniques such as planning and prioritising take effort and application which are not always associated with pleasure.

If you really want to improve, then you need to make a mental link between the effort involved and the pleasure that will come from working effectively. It may also mean that you have to get out of your comfort zone.

Read on ....

MANAGING WHAT YOU DO

- Job clarification
- Procrastination
- Setting priorities
- Estimating time
- Planning

A BUSY FOOL?

- Are your days filled with action from dawn till dusk?
- Would you say that you are busy?
- Are you **productive** or are you:
  - doing the things that you *like* doing, rather than the things that you *should* be doing?
  - putting your efforts into low-value activities rather than those that will give you a higher payoff for your efforts?
  - putting off what you know you should really be doing?

Many of us rarely stop and think about what we are doing and, more importantly, why we are doing it in the first place.

Start making changes to how you use your time by ensuring that you **focus your attention** on those things that matter.

This isn't easy. As already mentioned, we naturally fight to keep hold of those things that give us comfort, routine and enjoyment.

EFFICIENCY OR EFFECTIVENESS?

Central to time management is an understanding of the difference between efficiency and effectiveness.

- *Efficiency is doing things right* – following the rules, processes and systems that are in place

- *Effectiveness is doing the right things* – concentrating your attention on those things that need to be done in a particular situation **in order to produce results**

Very often we spend a lot of time on being efficient instead of concentrating on being effective - in other words doing the right things.

BEING CLEAR ABOUT YOUR JOB

JOB CLARIFICATION

If you are employed in a job you may have a job description explaining what you *have* to do. However, in a changing world what we *actually* do sometimes bears little or no similarity to our written job descriptions.

The idea of job clarification is a practical method that concentrates on the *results* to be achieved. Job clarification is:

- A shared understanding between you and your boss about:
  - what your job is
  - what you are expected to achieve
  - where/how it relates to other jobs

- A continual process reflecting changes in your knowledge and skills as well as in the job that you do and its priorities

- A way of saving time by concentrating your efforts on what's important. Without a clear understanding, how do you know what you should be spending your time doing?

JOB CLARIFICATION
HOW TO DO IT

Ask yourself:

- What's the purpose of my job?
- What am I there to achieve?

Example:

Overall purpose: To make money by developing existing and new business within the region at a profit.

Try to limit this statement to a single sentence.

JOB CLARIFICATION

IDENTIFYING KEY AREAS

Key areas are the main areas on which to concentrate your time and effort in order to achieve the overall purpose.

If you could split your job up into some main parts what would they be? For example, you might identify staff management, finance, projects, planning, research, training, customers, etc.

 Aim for a maximum of 8 key areas.

Key Areas

New Clients — Existing Clients — Performance Targets — Recruitment & Training

JOB CLARIFICATION
IDENTIFYING ACTIVITIES

Activities
- Are what you do in each key area eg:

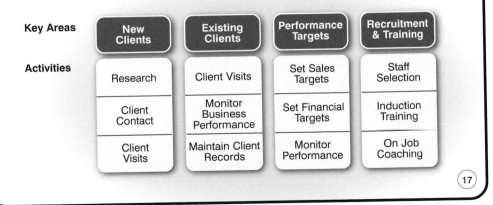

Key Areas	New Clients	Existing Clients	Performance Targets	Recruitment & Training
Activities	Research	Client Visits	Set Sales Targets	Staff Selection
	Client Contact	Monitor Business Performance	Set Financial Targets	Induction Training
	Client Visits	Maintain Client Records	Monitor Performance	On Job Coaching

JOB CLARIFICATION

OVERVIEW

Overall Purpose	To make money by developing existing and new business within the region at a profit		
Key Areas	**New Clients**	**Existing Clients**	**Performance Targets**	**Recruitment & Training**

Activities			
Research	Client Visits	Set Sales Targets	Staff Selection
Client Contact	Monitor Business Performance	Set Financial Targets	Induction Training
Client Visits	Maintain Client Records	Monitor Performance	On Job Coaching

Tip *Use job clarification to set objectives and agree priorities at appraisal time as well.*

HOW SHOULD YOU SPEND YOUR TIME?

How and where you spend your time can be influenced by many factors such as:

- Deadlines you may have to meet, around which you organise your time
- The degree to which you are told what to do and others decide how your time is spent
- The demands of customers, circumstances and events, to which you have to be flexible and responsive

As human beings we prefer doing the things that we enjoy rather than what needs to be done. We busy ourselves, and justify why we are doing low value activities, while putting off more challenging tasks.

It's called procrastination and is one of the biggest hurdles to making changes to the way we live our lives.

DO YOU PROCRASTINATE?

Most of us are in the habit of putting things off – it's just that some people do it better or more often than others. Do you delay dealing with the:

- Boring or routine task that is now a chore and not a challenge?
- Difficult phone call or decision that needs to be made?
- New job or project that you're unsure how to start?
- Individual who is making life difficult for you?

While it sometimes pays to delay certain jobs and weigh up the options, you know that sooner or later you will have to do them. It's amazing how much time, energy and creative thought can go into putting them off. If only that energy could be put into doing the job, not avoiding it – think how much easier your life might be!

The real danger is that we may never get round to doing things that really matter. We end up talking about what we're going to do, never do it and waste a lot of time in the process.

Tip *Don't put off until tomorrow what you should be doing today.*

MANAGING WHAT YOU DO

STOP PROCRASTINATING!

Take a job that you have been putting off...

- Do something (anything!) to make a start; visualise the pleasure you would gain from completing the job
- If it's a big job or project, break it down into smaller parts and do a little each day
- If it involves some form of creativity, do it when you are at your most energetic (see Prime Time on page 102)
- If it is a boring job (eg: filing) do it when you are at your least energetic
- Give yourself a *reward* at the end
- Try to break the habit of putting things off; problems are easier to handle when they're small and when they're recent

 Remember that the longer you put things off, the bigger the resistance to the task will become and the more difficult it will be to make a start.

WHAT TO DO FIRST?
SETTING PRIORITIES

Most of us have too much to do. How then do you decide what you should do and in what order? Typically we:

- Do things that we like doing – not what we need to do
- Usually start with the easy jobs that create a sense of satisfaction
- Think that we have to give priority to every job we are faced with
- Only realise the true priorities *(what's **really** important)* in life when we have a real problem to face

Ask yourself: *Is the job so important as to be a priority – should I do it?* If so:

- In which order should the jobs be handled?
- How much time should you give to each?
- When are you going to start?

PARETO (80/20 RULE)

If you have several jobs to do and are not sure where to start, the Pareto (80:20) concept could help you decide.

80% of Time Available → **20%** of the Results

20% of Time Available → **80%** of the Results

It suggests that a relatively small number of causes results in a large percentage of effects. In other words, some jobs are more productive than others. The secret is to know which ones they are and focus on them.

It could be that 20% of what you've got to do produces 80% of your results. These tasks give you a high return for your efforts.

On the other hand you may be spending 80% of your time on activities that only produce 20% of your results, not a good use of time!

 Tip *Concentrate on high payoff activities.*

(23)

DEALING WITH THE UNEXPECTED

- Unexpected events happen throughout the day and will affect what you plan to do
- Urgent jobs don't always have the highest payoff yet get priority over important ones
- Important jobs are the ones on which you should focus to be effective
- Use the model below to help prioritise when the unexpected crops up

IMPORTANCE

	Low	High
High (URGENCY)	Ask someone else to do it	Do it now – do it yourself
Low	Don't do it	Do it as soon as you can

THE IMPORTANCE OF A SYSTEM

- Think of a system as a discipline – a routine – that you get into
- Most successful people have a system for managing their time
- People who are good at multi-tasking are usually highly organised, in their own minds, though they may not use any manual system
- So what's the secret? Answer … there is none!

People who make good use of their time:
- Have worked out and developed a system that works for *them*
- Rarely – if at all – rely *exclusively* on any of the products that claim to be essential to time management (eg: a time method or the latest technological gadget)
- Use a system that *combines* their own ideas and those they have learned from others

DIARIES

A good diary can be an important part of any system you adopt. It provides practical benefits, such as:

- A record of what you plan to do and what has been achieved
- A source of information and reference
- A way of keeping control over your activities and life
- A prompt for those with poor memories

Many forms of diary system are readily available, from hand-held electronic devices and laptops to paper versions if you prefer to physically write down information. Choose what works for you.

Whatever you use, remember that it is an **aid** to managing time – do not let it rule your life. You still need the skills outlined in this book.

ESTIMATING TIME

The hardest time management skill to master is estimating the time a task will take. Why?

- You do not always know how long an activity will take until you get into it
- Interruptions (see pages 92-93 on dealing with them) break your concentration
- People, on whom you are relying, let you down
- Your available time is dictated by others, eg: customers who make their own demands

Underestimating can have implications for both you and others. Improve your chances by:

- Being realistic in your estimates (What does experience tell you? Will some jobs take longer than you expect?)
- Taking account of other demands in your work and in your life
- Asking 'What could go wrong?' (and never assuming that things will go to plan)

 As far as possible, always overestimate how long jobs will take.

THE IMPORTANCE OF PLANNING

If you want to achieve your goals, make good decisions or avoid pitfalls then planning is the key.

- Use job clarification to agree objectives and priorities for both jobs and projects
- Break large tasks into manageable chunks, each with their own timescale
- Work on turning these into actions by making detailed plans
- Identify what needs to be done, by whom and by when
- Use planning systems that are available, don't do everything in your head or as you go along
- Don't forget that plans can always be changed; however ...

IF YOU FAIL TO PLAN THEN PLAN TO FAIL

MANAGING WHAT YOU DO

THE DANGERS OF LISTS!

Often on time management courses you are encouraged to compile a daily *To Do* list.

In theory such a list helps you to:
- Convert bigger plans into smaller tasks
- Focus on what needs to be done thereby improving your productivity
- Gain a sense of achievement through the completion of a series of smaller tasks

In reality you could end up:
- With a list that's far too long – and varied – to ever achieve
- Having to transfer jobs from one day to the next
- Thoroughly demoralised at achieving very little on your list

Only write a list if it is linked to a specific task that you have to do (eg: organising a meeting, introducing a new procedure). This will act as a useful reminder. Don't, though, list every planned activity.

HOW TO ORGANISE YOURSELF

Everybody has their own way of working – what works for some doesn't work for others. Whatever you do:

- Be clear about what you are doing and why (Should you be doing it in the first place?)

- Try to arrange your work into manageable chunks or tasks to help you concentrate your mind and efforts

- Create a weekly or daily plan to give yourself:
  - sufficient lead-in time for major tasks
  - an overall picture, in case you need to change what you do (in response to those days when you achieve nothing!)

- Be realistic – you can only do so much in a day

- Review your plan throughout the day

- If the pressure is on consider what you can drop

 Put your efforts into key tasks every day - focus on payoff instead of urgency.

MANAGING WHERE YOU WORK

- Dealing with paper
- Filing
- Tips for regular travellers working on the move

ARE YOU SITTING COMFORTABLY?

Ergonomics is the study of the relationship between workers and their environment. A lot of thought goes into designing the layouts of the workplace so that people can be comfortable, safe, creative and productive.

- The space where you work is important – think of the amount of time you spend there

- Make sure that you have all the tools that you require close to hand. Think about the information you need, documentation, stationery. You could waste valuable time (almost 4 hours a week) having to stop and look for what you need

- Don't ignore where you sit. Have a comfortable well-designed chair and, if you use a computer, a desk at the right height plus adequate lighting

PAPERLESS OFFICE?

While some people are happy to work in a cluttered environment (and claim that they can lay their hands on any document you ask for) other people seem to have developed the skill of keeping their desks clear.

The problem with piles of paper is that the brain can only consciously focus on one piece of information at a time. The more clutter you have, the more you will be tempted to pick it up and look at it, especially if you are bored or procrastinating. It's a distraction from the work that you have to do.

Despite the development of technology many organisations and people still have in-trays and filing cabinets full of paper. Often it's a back up in case technology lets them down. It might also be a way of resisting fully embracing the opportunity of a new way of working.

DEALING WITH A CLUTTERED DESK

It is estimated that people with a cluttered desk could spend up to 45 minutes every day looking for lost papers or documents.

Cluttered desks aren't conducive to clear and creative thinking, so:

- Clear your desk of everything not related to what you're currently working on. This will help you to concentrate and focus your attention

- Resist the temptation to leave your current work on your desk

- Once you've finished a task, put all the papers relating to it away in a drawer, file or folder

- Always leave a tidy/clean desk when you go home at night – psychologically you'll come in refreshed the next day

- Adopt a system of dealing with paperwork (read on)

 Start by clearing your desk of all unwanted items.

HANDLE PAPER ONLY ONCE

Suggesting to people that they handle paper only once is often met with laughter.
The principle behind the suggestion, though, is sound – namely that you:

- Make a decision about every piece of paper that comes your way
- Avoid putting it down to *do later*
- Keep the flow of paper moving and not allow it to build up

When you receive papers:
- Read/decide what you want to do with it
- Apply the **GUTS** technique
  Give it away
  Use it
  Throw it away
  Send it
- Have a waste bin within easy range
- When it doubt, throw it out!

MANAGING INCOMING POST

If you are office based and do receive paper mail:

Incoming

- Look at the way you're organised and set up a system that works for you
- Stop unwanted items reaching you – remove your name from circulation lists (either internal or external)
- Deal with all mail that arrives on your desk:
  - hand write comments and pass it on
  - delegate it, or
  - dump it
- Handle your mail in a batch (all together) and deal with it accordingly
- Avoid setting up too many pending/miscellaneous/action trays – you'll only fill them with clutter
- Develop a system for allocating priorities to your mail, eg: A/B files (A: for action, B: to be read)

Outgoing

- Check all mail bearing your signature (it pays to!)

FILING SYSTEMS

- Whether setting up paper based or electronic files some basic principles apply, eg:
  - projects you are working on
  - routine jobs you perform daily, weekly, monthly
  - information required for meetings with key customers/staff
  - information needed at your fingertips (names, addresses, phone numbers, etc)
- For long-term pending or follow-through items, set up a *tickler* file; separate files represent each day of the month, behind are eleven folders for the months that follow
- Make sure that your files are clearly labelled
- If using a paper system, include a contents sheet (in a distinctive colour) inside the file. This will alert you quickly to what's inside and save you time. It will also help you decide what you *really* need the file to contain
- When setting up files electronically, search the internet as there are many excellent and innovative products to help save time and effort

FILE EVERYTHING!

Good advice but we know that filing is the most boring job in the world!

Useful tips:

- Cut down on the number of trays on your desk. What do you *really* need? If you never clear those pending trays or use the miscellaneous tray with all those papers that you haven't decided how to action, then get rid of them. Throw them out!
- Do your filing when you're at your least energetic in the day or the week
- Try putting all your filing in a pile and work through it systematically. As a rule of thumb, if you come across a piece of paper and you:
  - can't remember the last time you used it, and
  - don't know when you'll need it next - BIN IT!
  Put papers that you want to keep in a file and record in a diary or notebook where you put them

WORKING ON THE MOVE

If your work involves a lot of travelling, it is much easier than it used to be to work and stay in touch while on the move. But before you go anywhere, ask yourself if your trip is really necessary. Would an email, phonecall or web conference be a better use of your time?

If you do need to travel:

- Keep a checklist of everything you need to take, to speed up the packing process and provide reassurance that nothing vital has been forgotten
- Leave a copy of your itinerary in the office/at home for times when you cannot be contacted
- Carry a separate note of key phone numbers with you in case you have a problem with your mobile
- Jot down credit card numbers in a safe place
- Make sure you have your phone charger and adapters for using electrical equipment overseas

WORKING ON THE MOVE

- Set up a portable office: take your files, diary, laptop, mobile and charger with you
- Use travel time to catch up on reading or listening to podcasts, etc
- Try to avoid the herding instinct (standing in queues) at stations and airports
- Use the services of hotels for sorting out any problems
- Take the right clothes for both business and pleasure
- Minimise stress; after travelling, eat a light meal, get some exercise and, above all, try to relax
- Finally, never assume – anything!

MANAGING
YOUR COMMUNICATIONS

- Listening
- Handling phone calls
- Emailing
- Reading

- Writing
- Arranging meetings
- Chairing meetings

WHY IT IS IMPORTANT

- Communication is the life-blood of any organisation; without it we cannot exist
- Ours is a communication world: we can now contact anyone anywhere in the world at any time of the day
- We are bombarded with communication images from dawn till dusk
- Despite its importance it's still surprising just how careless people are when they are communicating – no wonder breakdown in communications is a major time waster in our lives
- With the emphasis on speed (often in place of attention to detail) we frequently make problems for ourselves by being careless and not considering carefully enough what and how we communicate

MANAGING YOUR COMMUNICATIONS

LISTENING – **THE** MOST IMPORTANT SKILL

Research indicates that we spend 80% of our day communicating; about half the time is spent listening.

An often quoted model (source unknown) would suggest that:

	Listening	Speaking	Reading	Writing
Order in which skills are learnt as children	1	2	3	4
% use as adults	45%	30%	16%	9%
Order in which we are taught	4	3	2	1

The message here is that listening is the first skill we learn as children, the one used the most, yet it is given the least attention in schools. Don't forget, there's a big difference between hearing and listening.

WHY DON'T WE LISTEN?

Most people hear - very few actually listen. Common mistakes include:

- Speed of thought: the brain can think faster than people can talk, thus we have plenty of spare time to criticise what's being said and plan our response
- 'Already listening' … 'I've made up my mind' … 'So why should I listen to you?'
- Outside distractions: phones, other conversations, people walking by
- Switching off when you hear unfamiliar jargon
- Wanting to speak and therefore inclined to interrupt
- Hearing what you expect to hear rather than the intended message
- Failure to put ourselves in other people's shoes
- Thinking we know what people are talking about
- Listening to the words but missing the music (emotions) behind them

Any of these sound familiar?

 Remember, most people you deal with aren't good listeners.

DIFFERENT KINDS OF LISTENING

- To listen you have to be involved
- We listen, for example, to:
  - be polite
  - obtain precise information
    (eg: directions or instructions)
  - find out more about the speaker
    or the topic
  - help our understanding of the other
    person's situation or ideas
  - find fault in what's being said
  - learn new ideas and approaches

 First be clear about why you're listening, then learn to pay attention.

45

HOW TO LISTEN

Recognise it's hard work and a skill for which most of us haven't been trained. Try:

- Remembering that – as an active skill – you need to be involved
- Taking notes (eg: mind maps) as a way of aiding memory retention
- Planning to tell someone else what you've heard – this way you will remember it better
- Being mentally present: pay attention and show interest in what people are saying
- Matching your behaviour to that of the speaker's (it's called *rapport* – being on the same wavelength). If you're listening to people on the phone, try to go at their pace – quickly or slowly
- Controlling your emotions; if you don't they will prevent you from listening effectively
- Avoiding distractions
- Being aware of when your mind starts to wander as you're obviously not fully listening

Listening is a skill and a gift – give it generously.

HOW TO LISTEN

- Recognise and acknowledge your own (bad) habits. Are there some people you never listen to?
- Pay attention and show interest in what people are saying (don't only listen to the words but try and pick up the emotions behind them)
- Be a *whole body* listener by using all your senses to listen to people's:
  - thoughts (all the words they say)
  - feelings (how ideas are presented)
  - intentions (what if anything they plan to do)
- Reflect back what you think they are saying. Try:
  - testing understanding: 'What do you mean by …?' and
  - summarising: 'So what you are saying is …'
- Finally, the most obvious one: keep your mouth shut and don't talk

 Active listening will save you time.

47

ASKING QUESTIONS

Asking questions (as a way of testing your understanding) is one way of demonstrating that you're listening. You can save time by asking skilful questions to get you the information you're looking for.

Closed questions (eg: 'Are you finding this book useful?') will give you only one answer.

WHEN?

WHERE?

WHAT?

Open questions (eg: 'How useful are you finding this book?') result in many possible answers. The questions usually start with 'who, what, why, when, where or how'.

Don't underestimate the skills and time-saving potential of asking questions. See *Interviewer's Pocketbook* by John Townsend, published by Management Pocketbooks, for a comprehensive guide to questioning techniques.

WHO?

HOW?

HOW THE PHONE HAS TAKEN OVER OUR LIVES

Phones make us accessible 24 hours a day.
They have become indispensible to us.

Time builds up, eg: 10% of your day on the phone,
whether speaking or texting, equates to:
- 6 seconds every minute
- 6 minutes every hour
- 40 minutes a day
- 3.5 hours a week
- over 2 days a month
- 24 days a year

If you don't believe these figures, use a
time log to record how long you spend
using your phone, or consult your bill.

MANAGING YOUR COMMUNICATIONS

PROS & CONS OF THE PHONE

Pros
- Practical, easy to use, any time, anywhere
- More personal than writing
- Gives immediate feedback
- Economical: you can make many calls in a short period of time
- On occasions can be quicker than email
- A well-timed call can save valuable time

Cons
- Lacks non-verbal aspects of face-to-face communication
- Receiver often unprepared for the conversation
- Can be costly and time consuming if you just ramble on
- Can interrupt and break your concentration
- Conversations can be overheard (especially when using a mobile)
- Can be difficult and time-consuming to get through to the right person (automated systems, voicemail, etc)
- You have no paper record of what has been discussed/agreed

USING THE PHONE FOR BUSINESS

Only use the phone when you **need** to. Remember that when using the phone for business, people will form an impression of you, your organisation and how your business is run.

- If possible, group your outgoing calls together and set aside time to make them
- Be prepared – have information ready for when people ring seeking answers to questions
- Speak clearly and slowly
- When making calls, be ready for an answer machine/voicemail
- When making mobile calls, choose your environment, eg avoid background noise and places where you know the signal is weak.

In general, use the phone to persuade when you have a stronger case than the other person (it minimises emotion and maximises objectivity when discussing the task at hand). In the case of a weak argument, avoid the telephone.

 Beware of giving away business sensitive information when making calls in public places.

GOOD PHONE TECHNIQUES

- Use a greeting – identify yourself and your location
- Don't just say 'Hello' or 'Hold on'
- Watch your manner – avoid signs of talking to others when you're meant to be listening
- Use your voice to add meaning through tone, pitch, inflection, etc
- Don't be afraid to tell people that they only have a fixed time – and stick to it
- Avoid answering the phone while you're eating or drinking
- Remember, people can't see you; your message is conveyed by your words and tones
- Sit up or, better still, stand up (this way you become more alert and attentive)
- Don't put pens in your mouth
- Smile (it's reflected in your voice)
- Concentrate on what's being said
- Make notes on key points (use mind maps to jot down what's said)
- Don't do other things and avoid the temptation to doodle
- Answer the phone quickly; don't let it ring and ring

MANAGING YOUR COMMUNICATIONS

DEVELOPING A CALLBACK SYSTEM

- There may be times when you have to brief others about calls that you are expecting in your absence. If so, let people know who might be calling:
  - why they are important
  - what the call might be about
  - what to say/how to handle the call
  - who you don't want to talk to – and why
- If you ask people to call back at certain hours make sure that you'll be there
- If the other person isn't there when you return a call don't feel obliged to keep trying if they're never in
- Make use of technological developments such as call waiting, pagers, text messaging and ring-back services
- If you're leaving a message for someone:
  - listen to the instructions on the machine before speaking
  - speak slower than you would normally, especially if giving contact numbers
  - tell people who you are and why you're phoning
  - make your message short to avoid getting cut off

IDEAS FOR MANAGING YOUR PHONE CALLS

- If you're required to hold, ask for how long
- Have a system for dealing with all incoming calls (helps the image)
- Use voicemail to help you manage your time, but don't overuse it as callers prefer to talk to a person not a machine
- Know before you call what you are going to say and get straight to the point
- Avoid weather reports (eg: 'What's it like up there?') and limit social chat
- If you have several non-urgent calls to make or return, save them up/group them together and make them just before lunch or towards the end of the working day, when people are more conscious of the time and less inclined to ramble on
- Don't forget that mobile phones – though convenient – aren't cheap
- Finally, if you've finished your business but the other person keeps going on and on (about the job, their home, their problems) then try cutting yourself off while you are talking (honest it works!!)

PROS & CONS OF EMAIL

ADVANTAGES

Emails and text messages have taken over our lives – how ever did we manage without them? With emails you can:

- Communicate at speed, with potential for quick response
- Go direct to the people who matter
- Cross continents and time zones
- Disseminate information to large numbers of people easily and quickly
- Send data files and pictures
- Control your own time better because you choose when to answer

PROS & CONS OF EMAIL

DRAWBACKS

Advantages aside, emails can be:

- Overwhelming unless there's a system for handling them
- A lazy option (there's sometimes no substitute for picking up the phone and talking to people – and it can be quicker)
- Difficult to detect the sender's emotions from the words and style of their writing
- Used by people to cover their backs by copying in all sorts of people
- A way of delaying decision-making as people keep asking questions or raising issues
- A distraction, especially if the computer *bleeps* every time a message arrives
- A pressure, because people expect an immediate response – or we think that they do

MANAGING YOUR COMMUNICATIONS

HANDLING EMAIL

Tips on dealing with paper (eg: handle it only once) don't always apply to electronic communications. Emails build up quickly so we have to find new ways of handling them. Useful tips include:

- Develop a routine for handling your mail, eg: set aside fixed times in the day (early morning, after lunch, last thing). This ensures a good response time and helps prevent messages from building up in your box

- Scan the headers and decide immediately which messages to delete. Although initially this may not be easy, with practice you will often find that the header and sender details will give you a clue as to whether the message can be ignored or is important

- Print only long emails that are important. Reading emails on the screen can be difficult, but don't print every message, only those that need time and consideration

- Set up folders to divert any unwanted junk mail

MANAGING YOUR COMMUNICATIONS

HANDLING EMAIL

- Explore the packages available to filter and file emails
- Organise your emails
  - set up folders and files to categorise your emails
- Do the shortest job first
  - select and deal with those you can get rid of first
- Keep answers short, clear and to the point
  - try to respond with simple phrases (yes, no, agree, sorry); long emails often get ignored
- Avoid the ping pong effect where messages go back and forth
- Get rid of old emails
  - create an archive folder to put them in

MANAGING YOUR COMMUNICATIONS

SENDING EMAIL

Necessary or not to send it?
- Is it relevant to people (especially if you are copying them in)?
- Does it repeat something people already know?
- Would a phone call be more effective, especially to establish initial rapport?
- Are you sending an email to protect someone (yourself?) rather than trying to achieve something?

Too long/too vague?
- Can the information be summarised in a few bullet points?
- Is it clear what action is expected and when? If not, either make it clear or do not send it
- Have you included your telephone number so that people can ring you if they prefer?
- Keep to a single topic per email – two short ones are better than one long 'catch-all' one

SENDING EMAIL

Avoid silly deadlines:
- Sending an email at the end of the day, asking for a reply by first thing on the following day is generally unreasonable
- When you need an urgent reply, telephone before sending the email or afterwards

Tone is important – avoid *flame mail:*
- Flame mail is email designed to criticise or ridicule the other person, usually sarcastic. However tempted you might sometimes feel, just don't do it. Also, writing in CAPITALS sets an aggressive tone
- If you need to send a reminder, try phoning
- Clipped phrases and language are okay, but check the overall tone
- Don't forget the rules of good writing and grammar; spelling/typing errors send out a message about you
- Keep your message short but include all the information necessary for others to act or respond (beware of sending too much)
- Read it through – would you be happy to receive it?
- *Please* and *thanks* add only a couple of words but mean a lot

MANAGING YOUR COMMUNICATIONS

READING EFFECTIVELY

If yours is a job that involves a lot of reading, knowing how to read and developing some simple techniques will save you valuable time.

Reading effectively improves your …
- Concentration
- Note-taking and memory
- … leading to better comprehension, retention of facts and better use of time

The first step towards effective reading is to decide what to read. In a business context this is usually governed by job priorities. Reading everything in detail can be a waste of time.
- Examine what's on your desk/screen – how much do you **really need** to read?
- Be ruthless: if you don't have to read it, then don't
- Set up a separate file for reading – but only if you know that you will be able to give it your attention, otherwise it will be yet another file cluttering your desk

READING QUICKER

When faced with a pile of reading, ask yourself if you are motivated to want to read it in the first place. If so, have you enough time to read and understand?

Preview what you have to read so as to prepare the mind and categorise the material. Skim the text and determine if it is:

- Important: if so, read it thoroughly
- Less important: skim and file/pass on
- Unimportant: reject and discard

If you are going to read it, decide your intentions. Will you, for example:

- Read it and file the copy for future use?
- Expect to be questioned on the contents?
- Have to write about it?

This influences your motivation and reading style.

MANAGING YOUR COMMUNICATIONS

IMPROVING YOUR READING SPEEDS

Do you take a long time to read documents or papers, struggle to understand words and, when you've finished, cannot recall what it was about? If so, give some serious thought to improving your reading skills, the basics of which are:

- Knowing the way your eyes function. Eyes jump from word to word in a series of short often erratic movements and do not flow smoothly over the text as you may think

- Understand how good written text is constructed, thereby picking out key words and passages

- Know why you are reading something in the first place. (Because you have to or because you want to?)

- Make your mind up about what to read/what not to read. Improve your personal organisation – clear your desk of distractions, get yourself comfortable

RAPID READING TECHNIQUES

There are some simple techniques that can significantly improve your reading speed and comprehension.

- Eye movements
  - use your finger or a pencil to guide your eyes over the text
  - don't fix or try to understand every word
  - fix on verbs, nouns and omit most other words
  - read spans (groups of words) and not individual ones

- Reveal techniques
  - use a card to reveal the lines one by one

- Don't go back over what you've read
  - if this is a habit, do the reverse of the previous suggestion: use a card to cover the text after you've read it

MANAGING YOUR COMMUNICATIONS

RAPID READING TECHNIQUES

- Overcome mental blocks
  - you *can* read faster, it is possible, and you'll improve your understanding and concentration
- Use different techniques
  - rapid reading (300-800 words per minute) for 60/70% comprehension by fixing on words/phrases
  - scanning/skimming (600-1,000 words per minute) for getting overall idea and locating information
- Practise
  - the more you read, the better you will become and the better your vocabulary will be; if your range of words is not good, don't be afraid to have a dictionary to hand (initially this may slow you up, but your vocabulary will be greater)

(See section on 'Reading' in *Use Your Head* by Tony Buzan, published by BBC Publications.)

Rapid reading techniques can dramatically improve your reading speeds and, ultimately, save you time.

GOOD READING HABITS

- Maintain a good posture – don't get too comfortable
- Hold book/papers at 45° in front of you, equidistant from eyes to desk
- Keep a clear workplace – or else your eyes will be distracted
- Set time limits on your reading – build up your time in stages
- Prioritise your reading
- Look for key ideas in first and last sentences of paragraphs

 Tip *Cut down your reading – get off unwanted mailing lists.*

MANAGING YOUR COMMUNICATIONS

WRITING: BE CLEAR WHY YOU'RE DOING IT

Even though we probably write more now using electronic means than we do with pen and ink, there's still no excuse for forgetting the basics of the written word. We write in order to:
- Transmit ideas and information
- Change ideas
- Sell, persuade or influence
- Gain ideas in response to what we write
- Record ideas and facts
- Amuse or impress

Don't forget the **K.I.S.S.** (**K**eep **I**t **S**hort and **S**imple) rule:
- Short sentences (less than 20 words)
- Simple words, short, no jargon
- No unnecessary words
- Short paragraphs, each linked to a main thought
- Short letters/memos/reports

 Be clear why you're writing in the first place.

ORGANISING YOUR WRITING

- Decide what you want to say
- Put it into a logical sequence
- Use a paragraph for each step
- Immediately identify the subject
- Keep your sentences short and to the point
- End by suggesting the way ahead
- Use punctuation to help understanding
- Use simple words and few of them

 Don't underestimate how long it will take you to compose and write a letter.

MANAGING YOUR COMMUNICATIONS

BASIC RULES FOR WRITING REPORTS

Things to consider:

- What's the purpose of the report?
- Who are the readers? (Who else might read it?)
- What do they know about the subject?
- What will prevent them understanding/accepting the report?
- Why will they be reading it?
- When/where will the report be read?
- Is it worth the time and effort?

 Again ... report writing takes time. Only write them if they are really necessary.

A STRUCTURE FOR REPORTS

If you decide that a report is needed then:

- Collect all materials
- Plan main parts of your report
- Select facts and group them under main headings
- Decide on layout
  - title
  - contents
  - summary of recommendations
  - main body of report
  - conclusions
  - appendices

TIPS FOR WRITING REPORTS

- If it's worth writing, it's worth writing well

- Use appropriate language (eg: don't use jargon if it will be read by non-specialists)

- A picture's worth a thousand words; so consider diagrams where appropriate:
  - graphs
  - charts
  - pictures
  - flow charts

 Try keeping your reports to a maximum of two A4 pages.

71

MEETINGS – A GOOD USE OF TIME?

Run properly meetings can be an effective way of:
- Communicating a message to a group
- Getting to know people
- Solving problems
- Drawing information from people's experiences
- Planning and making decisions
- Building teams

However, all too often meetings cause frustration because:
- There are too many of them
- There's no real purpose
- They're too long (one hour should be the maximum)
- They become a platform for the talkative
- Few decisions come out of them
- They make straightforward issues complicated
- They very often slow things down

*If you don't know
what you want the
meeting to produce,
don't hold it.*

MANAGING YOUR COMMUNICATIONS

MEETINGS ARE EXPENSIVE

The following figures are based on a working year of 240 days, with one working day equal to 8 hours. In some cultures the working week is less; however, with a trend towards contracting and self-employment the hours worked are often longer.

Salary p.a.	1 min	5 mins	10 mins	30 mins	1 hour	1 day
£50,000	43p	£2.17	£4.34	£13.00	£26.00	£208.00
£40,000	35p	£1.73	£3.47	£10.41	£20.83	£166.66
£35,000	30p	£1.52	£3.03	£9.11	£18.23	£145.83
£30,000	26p	£1.30	£2.60	£7.81	£15.63	£125.00
£25,000	22p	£1.08	£2.17	£6.51	£13.02	£104.16
£20,000	17p	£0.87	£1.74	£5.21	£10.42	£83.33
£15,000	13p	£0.65	£1.30	£3.90	£7.80	£62.50
£10,000	8p	£0.43	£0.86	£2.60	£5.20	£41.66

 Time is expensive – make meetings your last choice, not your first.

SUCCESSFUL MEETINGS

Characteristics of a successful meeting:

- Someone leads or takes the chair
- Starts on time
- There's a clear purpose/agenda and people are prepared
- People stick to the point and discussion is relevant to the topic
- Time limit (clear start and finish times)
- Agreed priorities and an effort to reach an agreement
- Few interruptions
- Regular summarising and an attempt by everyone to listen
- Rapid publication of results and further action

PLANNING YOUR MEETING

The following should be decided in advance:

- The purpose of the meeting: to give out information, share knowledge, solve a problem, negotiate? Planning, along with chairing, is key to effective meetings
- Who should attend. Don't invite people if the content is not relevant to them or they will not be able to contribute (maximum of fifteen people; 7-10 is manageable)
- Who, if at all, is required to make a special contribution. If there is a requirement, brief the person concerned beforehand so that they know what is needed and how long they have been allocated
- What is going to be discussed, why, when and how. (See next page on setting and following an agenda.)
- An agenda (a list of things to be covered) for both formal and informal meetings. Make sure people can understand it. Aim for a manageable amount of business to deal with (packed agendas create pressure and discourage calm discussion)

PREPARING AN AGENDA

People want to know what the meeting is about (beyond the title) and have time to prepare for it. Arrange the agenda in a logical sequence by:

- Deciding whether the items are for information, exploration, action or decision and how long each item will be allocated
- Creating a sense of achieving something by putting short easy items at the start
- Placing harder items in the middle when people are more alert
- Leaving brief *information only* items to the end
- Starting and finishing with an item involving everybody
- Not including items that could be dealt with by phone/memo/email (meetings are a chance to have face-to-face discussions)
- Using 3 P's for each item on the agenda to identify:
  - **Purpose**: why it is included (information, decision, action, etc)
  - **Process**: how it will be handled (eg: introduction by .. comments .. decision to be made on XYZ)
  - **Payoff**: what the benefits of discussing it will be
- Circulating the agenda beforehand wherever possible

ANY OTHER BUSINESS (AOB)

Even well run meetings can suffer from the AOB (Any Other Business) effect:

- AOB is often one of the most time-wasting parts of any meeting when people speak at length about often irrelevant topics
- If items are really that important then they should be on the agenda. If they are not, then a meeting is not the place to discuss them. Do it some other way
- If it is really necessary to discuss AOB as part of the meeting, then do not put it at the end where there is a real danger that it will drag the meeting out
- Put AOB at the start and give it an allocated time (say 10 minutes). In so doing you're giving it a defined time limit so as not to take away people's thoughts and energy from the main business of the meeting that follows

CHAIRING MEETINGS

- A good chairperson shapes the meeting. Their involvement in composing the agenda is vital to the meeting's outcome and success
- Start on time: this not only gives you a chance of finishing on time but sends a clear message to others about what you expect. Always have a clock visible
- By always starting promptly, people soon take good timekeeping for granted. Make it a rule of your meetings and people will appreciate it
- Waiting for latecomers merely rewards poor timekeeping. Those who are there on time will feel punished if you insist on waiting
- Handling latecomers can be tricky and demands diplomacy. You need to be welcoming and make it easy for the person to join in. Indicate the point the meeting has reached and summarise any important decisions made
- Introduce each item on the agenda: remind people of the 3 P's (see page 76)
- If you introduce an item that requires a decision, make sure that the meeting knows in advance what method will be used, eg: consensus (all contribute), majority, expert (go with their recommendations). Above all, there should be no surprises!
- Introduce a rule about use of mobiles during the meeting

CHAIRING MEETINGS – GIVE PEOPLE A ROLE

As chair you don't have to do everything yourself. Apart from the obvious – delegating minute-taking – there are other ways to reduce your workload:

- Construct the agenda carefully so that certain items may be led by others
- Delegate timekeeping, especially to someone who has a habit of turning up late. Get them to tell you when there are 5 minutes left for a particular item
- Ask somebody to act as a summariser for a particular agenda item. Rotate this role to keep people on their toes, including yourself. This will ensure that you or other members don't get bored!
- Encourage people to leave their chairs occasionally and move around. This usually raises energy levels and changes the dynamics of the meeting
- Experiment with using a flip chart to record people's ideas (another role that can be delegated), posting sheets around the room
- During the meeting remind people of the progress. It discourages repetition and allows you to refer to previous points (keeps meeting on track)

 If you want to hold a really short meeting use a room without chairs; business will be concluded remarkably quickly!

GETTING THE MOST OUT OF YOUR MEETINGS

If people are taking up valuable time by:	Deal with it by:
Waffling	*Asking them to summarise*
Being negative about what is being said	*Getting a positive comment from them*
Talking while others are speaking	*Saying 'One meeting please … can you share your ideas through the chair'*
Trying to dominate	*Saying 'That's interesting… what do others think?'*
Losing interest and wandering off the point	*Giving them a job to do*
Side-tracking the meeting	*Summarising and bringing the meeting back to main theme*
Arguing with others in the meeting	*Getting them to summarise how they see things from their point of view*

Managing to work with others

- Working with your boss
- Teamworking
- Interruptions
- Assertion
- Saying 'No'
- Asking for help

WHY IT'S IMPORTANT

If you work in an organisation there may be times when you think that life would be easier if you simply worked for yourself. No longer the demands of the boss, the moods and problems of colleagues, the constant interruptions, to say nothing of the politics and difficult customers.

Few of us work alone in the true sense. Even those of us who are *independent* still have to work with customers/suppliers, have projects to organise and deadlines to meet.

Work today does not necessarily involve going to an office. More people work from home as part of a virtual or remote team. This in itself calls for a wide range of skills, technology being just one of them. (See *Virtual Teams Pocketbook*.)

MANAGING TO WORK WITH OTHERS

WORKING WITH YOUR BOSS

A boss can be somebody you report to or somebody you work for, eg: a client.

Whoever they are, they can be the cause of frustration, stress and time-wasting. Many of us complain about our bosses. It's not until you are in their seat that you realise what a difficult job they have.

If you waste time complaining about your boss or believe there's little you can do to change the relationship, remember:
- You are 50% of the relationship
- You are 100% in control of your own behaviour
- You have a lot in common, eg: you both have:
  - a job to do and depend upon each other to do it
  - personal goals, needs, aspirations, strengths and weaknesses
- Your boss relies on you to produce results; if you're good then he or she will often want others to see the product of your efforts

YOU AND YOUR BOSS: WHAT'S THE DIFFERENCE?

Boss has (arguably):

- Greater status
- Easier access to powerful people and wider influence
- More command of resources
- Greater knowledge of the bigger picture (knows what's going on)

You (may) have:

- Greater knowledge of day-to-day situations
- More up-to-date information & better technical skills
- Closer customer contact
- Easier access to the team and what's really happening

In other words, you're not completely powerless. The secret is to recognise what each person brings to the relationship and build on it, not for each side to complain about each other and any weaknesses.

MANAGING TO WORK WITH OTHERS

GET TO KNOW YOUR BOSS

If you want to handle your boss you'll have to know more about him or her as a person.
However, this is not as easy as it may sound since, increasingly, we have more than one boss.

- How did they get the job?
  - Where did they work before and what did they do?
  - What are they hoping to achieve in their present job?

- What are they good at – where are they *not so good*?
  - What do they like/dislike doing?
  - Are they good with ideas or rely on others to do the thinking?

- What is their working style?
  - Do they prefer written or verbal reports, like formal meetings, want to be presented with solutions, or like to know all the facts and options available?

- What are their circumstances?
  - What are the pressures on them?
  - How do they get on with their own boss?
  - What else is happening in their lives?

WORKING WITH YOUR BOSS

Try to develop a relationship that lets your boss know you can be relied upon both to do your job and be supportive.

- Be available
- Try and see things through the eyes of your boss
- Impress on them that you're doing a good job
- Look for ways of using any of your strengths to compensate for any of their weaknesses
- When delegated a job, do your best and see it through to completion; if in doubt, ask for help and guidance – sooner rather than later
- Get involved and keep close; find out what they are working on
- Don't rely on them for constant guidance; you can provide:
  - ideas and alternative ways of doing things (you're often closer to what might be happening)
  - your views of the problems and situations

HOW BOSSES CAN STEAL YOUR TIME

Whatever you do, don't allow the boss to steal your time by being:

- Hard to get hold of:
  - if they have a secretary, find out when they are free
  - try contacting them by email or via their mobile
  - drop a note explaining that you've been trying to make contact

- Slow to respond to requests:
  - explain why it's important that a quick reply is needed
  - use colleagues to remind them
  - make it easy for them to say yes by outlining the options and offering recommendations

- Vague in their communications:
  - ask for clarification at the time
  - repeat back what you think he or she has said/asked for
  - tell them what you are going to do as a result of what you think you have heard (listening skills again)

HOW BOSSES CAN STEAL YOUR TIME

Bosses can steal your time by:

- Making unrealistic demands. If so:
  - explain how you feel about it at the time
  - remind them about your other current workload (ask *them* to prioritise what's important)
  - say 'No' (see pages 98-99)

- Not telling you what's going on. If so:
  - remember that there might be a valid reason for this (politics or something you have done)
  - try using your connections to find out what's happening
  - confront them; be assertive – tell them how you feel

- Being inconsistent. If so:
  - remind them of any decisions made/policies, etc
  - try and find out why – it may be an organisational problem/difficulty
  - keep a diary of what happens – or doesn't happen – especially if it's becoming a habit

MANAGING TO WORK WITH OTHERS

BEING PART OF A TEAM

Increasingly, people are working as part of a team. In fact, you may belong to several teams working on a whole range of projects. The belief is that teams have the potential to achieve more than individuals working alone. However, successful teams don't happen overnight.

Sadly, because of what happens when groups of people try to work together for the first time, much energy is taken up with:

- Deciding how to get organised
- Agreeing who should lead the group
- Resolving potential conflicts about who does what, how decisions will be made, what people can and can't do
- Getting to know what each member of the team can contribute

The result is that a lot of time can be spent in what might appear to be unproductive discussions. However, with any team it's vital that basic decisions are made to ensure the team's future success. Unfortunately, though, this can be time consuming.

TIME-SAVING TIPS FOR TEAMS

Should you be asked to join a team, be clear about why you have been nominated. If you're good, your skills, experience and time will be sought by others. With all your other commitments consider whether you can spare the time. If not, then you owe it both to yourself and the team to say 'No'.

If you agree to join then make sure that your team:
- Has a clear brief as to what is expected, to what standard and by when (this will give you a focus)
- Understands the priority of the task you are working on
- Knows how long you will be expected to devote to the task and the implications for your other work (often you will still be expected to do your *normal* work as well)
- Fully appreciates each member's contribution and recognises what they can offer (not only is it a waste of valuable time but it is also a crime to have talent available and not use it)

Remember that teams are only needed when there's a need to tackle real problems where nobody knows the answer. Don't waste time trying to be a team if you don't need to be one.

MANAGING TO WORK WITH OTHERS

SAVE TIME BY LEARNING TO CO-OPERATE

- When you have your team meetings, make sure that your goal (or what you want to achieve) is visible for all to see. Use it to re-focus where necessary
- If you've set any team rules (eg: *start and finish on time; if you disagree with what is said, then always offer a better solution*) make them visible and refer to them as and when required
- To achieve effective use of time and resources, rotate the leadership to people who may be better qualified for certain activities
- Learn to recognise what happens in groups: much time is wasted when people gang up on one another, play politics and put their own interests above the needs of others. Don't be afraid to point this out if you see it happening
- Allow people to *let off steam* where necessary and share with others how they are feeling. Progress can often be held back when people can't express their concerns and opinions
- Encourage fun and laughter. After all, people are more productive when they enjoy their work and hardly notice the passing of time

RECOGNISING INTERRUPTIONS

Where do interruptions come from? Do any of the following sound familiar?

Boss interrupts you with a change of plan and even more work.

Subordinates take advantage of your good nature and availability at any time of the day … or night.

Colleagues think you have all the time in the world to chat even though this is far from the case.

Clients and customers make demands, interruptions you can't afford to ignore!

Phone rings constantly, and text messages arrive at all times of the day and night.

Emails that bleep with every message.

Remember, interruptions blow you off course but they can be managed … read on.

Tip

MANAGING TO WORK WITH OTHERS

HANDLING INTERRUPTIONS

- When you're interrupted, ask yourself: 'What's more important, the interruption or what I'm working on?'
- Keep a list of current jobs. This will help you to re-focus on what you should be doing once you've handled the interruption
- Try to keep interruptions short: 'What do you want, why, when?'
- Keep a log of who/what interrupts you; a pattern may emerge of who interrupts and on what subjects
- Be assertive; learn to deal with: 'Have you got a minute?'
- Invent a deadline
- Continue to look busy:
  - stand up to interruptions: people rarely sit down while you are standing
  - remove the spare chair in front of your desk
  - reduce or, even better, avoid eye contact
  - collect your papers, check your watch
- Go to them – this way you can leave any time
- Learn to say 'No' (read on for suggestions)
- Plan a quiet hour if you're really that busy and don't want to be interrupted

MANAGING TO WORK WITH OTHERS

LEARN TO BE ASSERTIVE

If you believe that everybody has the right to interrupt you and that you can't say 'No', then you will always fall victim to other people's demands on your time.

Being assertive is behind many of the suggestions for dealing with interruptions. Assertiveness is standing up for your rights without disregarding the basic rights of others.

By being assertive you:
- Are fair to yourself and others
- Stand up for your rights and your point of view
- Let other people know where you stand

Learn to be assertive when:
- You are not afraid of revealing your feelings to others
- You want to achieve a win/win situation
- You've developed some skills and confidence
- People are stealing your time

MANAGING TO WORK WITH OTHERS

HOW TO BE ASSERTIVE

- First of all, recognise that you have the basic human right not to be taken for granted by others – you owe it to yourself to respect yourself and what you stand for
- Stop telling yourself negative thoughts – if you feel that you're unworthy or afraid of upsetting people then it will show in how you behave
- Start recognising and telling yourself what you are good at. Practise *self-affirmations* – in other words, positive statements about yourself that lead to assertive behaviour
- Act confidently, stand upright, keep eye contact, relax your body and avoid nervous gestures
- Speak with a clear voice and be direct – don't make excuses or start off by apologising
- Use 'I' statements as a way of telling people how you feel and/or what you want
- Be specific – words such as *might* and *maybe* suggest indecision; *should* and *will* are more demanding and are aggressive in tone
- Finally, listen to what people are saying, stay calm and use summarising to avoid any misunderstandings

MANAGING TO WORK WITH OTHERS

BEWARE OF MONKEYS!

A measure of your assertiveness is the extent to which you can both spot and deal with monkeys!

Monkeys are other people's problems that somehow end up on your back. Despite being a busy person, it is easy to get sucked into doing things for others. Often requests for your time (beware, monkeys frequently arrive by email) have little or nothing to do with your job.

Whatever the reason, each time you say 'Yes' to any request you collect another monkey – someone else's problem. What's more, monkeys eat into the time you have got to yourself after meeting the demands of your boss and job.

HANDLING MONKEYS

Taking the monkey often means that you are taking on a problem. As long as you are dealing with it others will not bother to take the initiative or sort it out themselves. To handle monkeys:

1. Deal with them as they happen. Say 'Yes, I can help' (beware what you may be taking on) or 'No, I cannot' (remember to be assertive).
2. Do not allow them to become too many – they will weigh you down in addition to everything else.
3. Handle them face-to-face only or by phone (avoid emails or texts).
4. Tell people you're too busy and invite them to come back at a certain time (it's amazing how many people don't come back!).
5 Suggest an alternative person who might be better able to deal with their situation.

 Never say 'Leave it with me'. If you do, you will have picked up a monkey and people will expect you to solve the problem.

SAYING 'NO'

Doubtless you can all recall situations when you have said 'Yes' to something only to regret it later. What's more, you know you should have said 'No' in the first place!

While other people may say 'No' to us, we find it difficult to say the same to them. Saying 'No' is one of the most difficult things to do. Despite being able to say 'No' when we are young children, most of us grow up to be people pleasers and rarely use the word 'No'.

While it is sometimes a compliment to be asked for your time and assistance, you will only feel bitter if you say 'Yes' when you should have said 'No'.

If your approach is non-assertive and accompanied by weak excuses you could get found out; if you're aggressive it could come out as an attack on the other person. The secret is to make sure your voice is firm and direct. Look into the other person's eyes as you say 'No'. Shake your head as you are saying it as well. And don't back down later.

SAYING 'NO'

If you always say 'Yes' to every request, then you'll never be able to manage your time. You'll always be giving it away to others. 'No' is a creditable response. Remember that you say 'No' to a request and not a person.

- If you're asked to do something less important than your current task (or simply do not want to do something) you need to say: 'No'. 'No, I can't'
- Don't apologise, so don't start your reply by saying: 'I'm sorry ...'. It will only make you feel guilty
- If necessary, use the broken record technique: repeat your answer several times (this will wear people down and means you do not have to think very hard under pressure)
- Be direct: 'I appreciate you asking me, however, I can't help you at present'
- If you're in the habit of saying 'Yes' and regret it afterwards, try giving yourself time to think: 'I need to check my diary – ask me again later'
- Don't feel that you should give a reason
- Stay calm: avoid getting emotional or sounding annoyed or frustrated
- If your boss makes the request say: 'This is what I am working on at present. Which one do you want me to drop in order to fit in your request?'

MANAGING TO WORK WITH OTHERS

ASKING FOR HELP

Talk to people in organisations about delegation and they usually laugh. Increasingly, they are being asked to achieve more with fewer resources and within tighter deadlines. Nowadays there aren't the people around to delegate jobs to.

Yet, with the emphasis on teamworking, asking for help is a justifiable action. So:
- Don't feel guilty or apologise about asking
- Be clear about what help you want, why and when
- Try and see things from the other person's point of view: 'What's in for them?'
- Vary your styles:
  - Informal: 'Would you do this when you have the time and opportunity please?'
  - Collaborative: 'I know you've got most experience in the team, I'd appreciate your help'
  - Problem focused: 'I have a problem that needs some fresh thinking. Would you help me with this?'
- Practise what you preach: be prepared to help others when you have the time
- Finally, don't hold it against people if they say 'No'. They may have already read this book!

MANAGING EVERY DAY

- Prime time
- Taking control
- Problem solving
- Mind mapping
- Making decisions
- Stress

PRIME TIME

- We all have a *prime time* during the day when we're at our best and fully alert
- The secret is to recognise this and do those activities that require energy, application and thought when you're at your sharpest
- When energy is low, we are sluggish and tend to make mistakes
- Watch what you eat: a heavy meal and wine make a lot of people lethargic; a healthy meal can provide energy for hours
- Work in periods of time (a maximum of an hour before taking a break) – this way you'll concentrate better

 Don't waste high-energy time doing low-priority work.

TAKING CONTROL

Better time management involves taking more control over what you do at work and home. However, this is not as easy as it sounds. Each day things happen to us over which we have little or no control.

- Customers make demands that need to be met
- Meetings are called by others; the timings and lengths of which can be unpredictable
- People go on holiday and their jobs have to be covered
- Accidents and emergencies occur that need our immediate attention
- Machines and systems (especially computers) breakdown and disrupt our plans
- Sickness can affect us all at any time
- Getting from A to B often takes longer than expected (increased traffic!)
- Natural disasters occur

What is left is the amount of time to do what you plan to do. Is it enough?

TAKING CONTROL

The amount of time you can control is influenced by:

Your job
If you are there to provide a service to customers, then your day will be full of interruptions.

Your boss
The more demanding, unpredictable and disorganised your boss is, the more likely he or she will influence how you spend your time.

Yourself
If you want to be everyone's friend, then you will give away time to those who want to steal it (remember monkeys?). If you're serious about wanting to take control over your life:

- Start saying 'No' to people (see pages 98-99)
- Learn to handle interruptions (see page 93)
- Develop a better working relationship with your boss (see pages 85-88)
- If things are getting too much for you then learn to manage the stress of it all (see pages 118-123)

PROBLEM SOLVING

Most of the problems we face every day we solve without giving them a moment's attention. However, the word *problem* itself can cause negative thoughts that drain energy, create panic and take up a lot of time.

There are situations where something has happened (eg: printer has run out of ink, a light bulb has blown). Then it's simply a question of fixing it – problem solved. We know that over time both of these items (ink/bulb) will have to be replaced.

There are other situations where the cause is unknown (eg: your car breaks down or you have a system failure on your computer). More investigation is needed to find the cause.

Sometimes we deal with a problem only to find that it keeps recurring. This is often because we have dealt with the symptoms and not got to the root cause. Adopting a structured approach can shed new light on a problem or situation and eventually save you time.

IDENTIFYING THE PROBLEM

Useful questions to ask when problems occur are:

- Who/what is the problem?
- What isn't it?
- Where is the problem?
- Where isn't it?
- When is it a problem?
- When isn't it?
- How big is the problem?

Methods for finding the cause of the problem and not just the symptoms include application of the *Cause* and *Effect* (sometimes known as *Fishbone*) diagram, See online for templates.

Place the problem statement (effect) on one side, identify the major cause categories, then look to break down each of the causes. Recurring causes could give the clue to the root cause.

Learn to get to the core of problems and not simply address/deal with the symptoms.

PROBLEM SOLVING – CAUSE & EFFECT TECHNIQUE

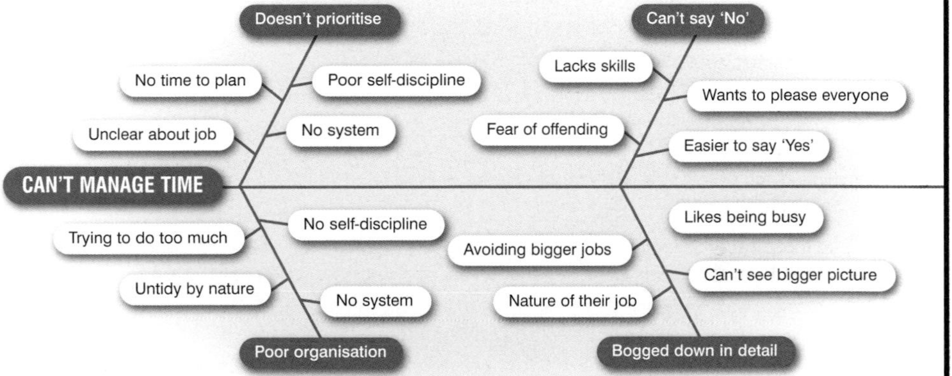

BEING CLEAR ABOUT THE PROBLEM

A well-defined statement of the problem (reflecting the root cause) can save you time and help focus your thoughts/energies. It should be:

- Stated in short and precise words
- Clear and unambiguous
- Able to be measured

 Tip *If you're stuck, try starting with the words 'How to ...'*

How will you measure success?

In simple terms there are normally two types of criteria for success:

- Musts… are the essential conditions that need to be met
- Wants … are the desirables after the musts have been satisfied

MANAGING EVERY DAY

GENERATING IDEAS FOR PROBLEM SOLVING

We are sometimes faced with problems that we haven't tackled before. These require us to challenge our assumptions and usual way of thinking. We need to stimulate creativity and fresh insights in ourselves and in others. Try:

- Talking to others – after all, you may not be the only one with the problem
- Consulting experts: What would they do?
- Looking at the problem from a different angle
- Describing it another way
- Challenging all you know about the problem
- Forcing out the real issues by continually asking: 'Why?'
- Using your experience: What does it tell you about such situations?
- Leaving it 24 hours ... see what it looks like then

MIND MAPS TO AID CREATIVITY

Mind maps are ways of pooling thoughts and generating free-thinking ideas on a topic, usually in diagrammatic form (sometimes known as spider diagrams, brain patterns).

Use the principles for:
- Creating ideas and insights into problems (do a mind map, leave it for 24 hours and re-visit it to see what you can add to your original thoughts)
- Compiling reports
- Taking notes at a meeting or during a phone call
- Planning presentations

Advantages over ordinary list-making:
- Can be built on
- New information is easily added
- Links between ideas are easier to see
- Helps recall

DRAWING MIND MAPS

- Use a large sheet of paper or on-line software
- Put theme/topic in centre
- Branch out with ideas from the centre
- Print your words on the lines
- Jot down what comes into your head – until ideas dry up
- Don't worry about the order of presentation
- Use different colours for different ideas

TECHNIQUES FOR SOLVING PROBLEMS

While people may be familiar with brainstorming, other techniques for groups include:

- **Trigger sessions** – in which each individual is given a set of cards or *post-it* pads and encouraged to generate ideas to a stated problem. These are then shared with the group, who look for links to suggestions already made by others

- **Analogy** – where a person tries to draw a likeness between a problem identified in one type of business with a proven solution in another

- *Wildest idea or get fired* – where individuals are encouraged to come up with answers that are so crazy that their colleagues would be seriously concerned about their sanity if they were suggested in a meeting. From a ridiculous starting point the group then try to develop potentially practical solutions

- **Defect analysis** – in which the group are encouraged to find what is wrong with a product, service or situation and create solutions for each defect listed

 Don't always stick to brainstorming when trying to solve problems.

CHOOSING THE BEST SOLUTIONS

Having generated ideas and possible ways ahead:

- Compare them against the criteria of *musts* and *wants*
- Go with any solutions that meet the *musts* (essential) criteria (the *wants* are desirable and are often a bonus)
- Now explore the implications of going with the ideas you have come up with:
  - What may it mean in practice?
  - How are you going to make it happen?
  - Who else has to be involved and what are the implications?
  - What do you need to do and in what order?
  - What would happen if it went wrong? Have you a fall-back position?
  - Can you have a trial run?
  - How long will it take?

MAKING DECISIONS

Not only do we spend time solving problems we also spend time making decisions, some major, a lot routine. There's no such thing as a *right* decision, yet we can learn from every decision we make, be it *good* or *bad*.

When making a decision bear in mind:
- The amount of time you have available
- That stress and emotion can affect the decisions you make
- Decisions made on *gut reaction* need to be supported by evidence
- That you can limit your choices by relying on what you did before and not exploring fresh ways and ideas
- What has happened in the past will not necessarily happen in the future
- Events don't always work out as you planned or hoped for … so expect things to go wrong

MAKING DECISIONS

You can save time by having:

- A clear picture of what you're trying to achieve (see problem solving tips)
- A thorough understanding of the situation/problem
- As many facts as you are able to gather
- Jotting down the pros and cons of any decision you've got to make
- People prepared to take a risk (especially when you don't have all the information)
- Sound judgement (you've weighed up all the pros and cons)

DOES YOUR MEMORY LET YOU DOWN?

Do you waste time trying to remember where you left papers, or what you should be doing or the names of people you meet? In short, have you a problem with your memory?

- Every day we remember thousands of things, yet it is not uncommon for people to say they have a bad memory
- Our memories have amazing capacity
- Memory can improve and not decline with age if it is used or developed
- Moderate drinking will not destroy brain cells; only excessive drinking will
- Our problem is not the capacity to take in information, it's the ability to recall what is in our heads
- You can develop the skills to remember names, faces, phone numbers and what you've learnt; see *Use Your Memory* by Tony Buzan (BBC Publications) for practical help or *Memory Pocketbook* by Vicki Culpin (Management Pocketbooks)

 If you have problems with your memory try learning some simple techniques.

IMPROVING YOUR MEMORY

- To improve we have to use both sides of the brain (the logical and creative sides)
- If you have problems with remembering then write things down in diaries or planners
- Pay attention to what you are doing … slow down … try and make links with what you hear, see and do
- Try mnemonics such as colour coding, highlighting, underlining, mind maps, spider diagrams
- If you can't recall where you put things:
  - have a mental parking space for everything
  - make visual associations based on images, symbols, tunes, letters, etc
  - relate what you want to remember to what you were doing at that time
- If remembering names is a problem:
  - pay careful attention when you first meet
  - try and make a link between their name and what is special/unique about them
  - ask them to repeat their name if you haven't heard it correctly first time
  - reinforce your new found knowledge by repeating their name in any conversation you have with them, so as to strengthen the association

STRESS – WHEN IT ALL GETS TOO MUCH

The fact that you're reading this book would indicate that you either have an interest in making better use of your time or that time is a problem. It could be that the stress of daily life is having an effect. After all:

- Evidence is emerging of people working long hours, thereby putting health and family relationships at risk

- Pressures to compete and meet ever-increasing demands of customers (as well as the need to hang on to a job) are forcing people to spend more of their time working

- While stress does have its benefits, too much can cause errors of judgement, mistakes, accidents and damage to health

- Some people are more vulnerable to stress from overwork than others; American researchers identified two types of individuals – Type 'A' who, though thriving on stress, are vulnerable to its effects, and Type 'B' who rarely let events disturb them

- Not only are there Type 'A' people but, one suspects, also Type 'A' organisations – read on to see if yours is one of them

STRESS – TYPES A & B

Type A
- Focus on output, achievement and results
- Are concerned with speed, performance and productivity
- Tend to be aggressive, impatient, intolerant, driving themselves and others hard
- Are preoccupied with time, go from appointment to appointment
- Are eager to start and finish on time
- Are strong, competitive (winning is crucial)
- Believe success is all that matters – which creates stress and pressure in others
- Are prone to heart attacks

Type B
- Are relaxed and easy going
- Take difficulties and problems in their stride
- Like to spend time on what they're doing
- Are rarely harassed or flustered
- Take time to ponder alternatives
- Usually feel there's plenty of time to do things
- Lead a balanced life … don't live to work
- Are less prone to heart attacks

STRESS – WHAT IS IT?

- Popular definitions include: *the result of a person being pushed beyond the limit of their natural ability*

- When used in physics, stress is defined as: *the external pressure applied to an object*

- Resultant change is called *strain*

- Applied to people, we mix up the two terms, using *stress* to refer to both the pressures we're under and the effect it has on us

Note *Not all 'stress' is harmful.*

STRESS – CAUSES

Where you work
Legislation, changes, demands from customers, rumours and office politics

The job that you do
Volume of work (too much/little), deadlines, pressures, being responsible for staff

Your career to date
Drifting along with no clear goals, not really enjoying what you do, seeing no possibility of change, uncertain future

Your relationships
Tension with people at work, friends, partner, boss, staff, children and families

Conflicts
Unable to find a balance between work and home; financial worries

Self-imposed
Give yourself a hard time, low self-image, poor self-management

STRESS – RECOGNISING SIGNS

Physical
Headaches, indigestion, throbbing heart, allergies, infections, twitching, nausea, tiredness, weight loss/gain, vague aches and pains

Mental
Indecision, making mistakes, forgetfulness, poor concentration, easily distracted, worrying more, making hasty decisions

Emotional
Irritability, anger, alienation, nervousness, apprehension, loss of confidence, tension, cynicism, job/life dissatisfaction

Behavioural
Unsociable, restless, unable to unwind, appetite loss/gain, diminished/increased interest in sex, increase in drinking/smoking, taking work home, too busy to relax, poor management

STRESS – HOW TO REDUCE IT

Remember, you have a choice – do nothing, fight it or learn to manage it by:

- Identifying what causes you stress and how it shows itself (this will give you a clue about what you need to tackle)
- Concentrating on what must be done and cutting out all those non-essential meetings, phone calls and visitors
- Learning to ask others for help; none of us is indispensable
- Pacing yourself; have 10 minute breaks throughout the day
- Being tidy and organised; untidiness creates its own problems
- Learning to say 'No' – don't take on everything that comes your way
- Eating properly, avoiding too much fat and sugar
- Improving your listening skills; many busy and energetic people are bad listeners
- Taking breaks – make sure you use all your holiday entitlement
- Keeping fit – try swimming and/or walking
- Learning to manage your time more effectively

WHERE NOW ...?

- Accept that you'll never have all the time you need to do what you want
- Understand that lack of time is often a symptom of other problems (taking on too much, poor planning, can't say 'No')
- Remember that if things are **really** important you'll find the time – from somewhere

So:
- Build on what works for you
- Don't set out to make dramatic changes to the way you operate – try new ideas gradually
- Try working smarter and more effectively (working longer doesn't mean that you'll be more productive!)
- Above all, if managing time is a problem for you, do **something** (hopefully with the help of this book)

FURTHER READING

There are numerous books on time management, the majority of which promote the same messages about prioritising and organising. What is not often covered in depth are the skills you'll need.

The Management Pocketbook series has a comprehensive range among which you will find the following useful for improving your time management:

The Assertiveness Pocketbook
  by Max A Eggert
The Business Writing Pocketbook
  by Clive Bonny
The Coaching Pocketbook
  by Ian Fleming
The Communicator's Pocketbook
  by Sean Mistéil
The Decision-making Pocketbook
  by Neil Russell-Jones
The Emotional Intelligence Pocketbook
  by Margaret Chapman

The Improving Efficiency Pocketbook
  by Philip Holman and Derek Snee
The Influencing Pocketbook
  by Richard Storey
The Stress Pocketbook
  by Mary Richards
The Teamworking Pocketbook
  by Ian Fleming
The Telephone Skills Pocketbook
  by Mary Richards
The Virtual Teams Pocketbook
  by Ian Fleming

About the Author

Ian Fleming, MA DMS Dip Ed
Ian works as a coach with individuals and teams helping
them achieve results by raising their level of performance
and confidence.

Should you want to talk to Ian about his ideas and approach,
contact him at:
'Summer Bank', 38 Abbey Road, Llandudno, North Wales LL30 2EE.
Tel. 01492 877539   email: ian@creativelearning.uk.com

Pocketbooks – *available in both paperback and digital formats*

360 Degree Feedback*
Absence Management
Appraisals
Assertiveness
Balance Sheet
Body Language
Business Planning
Career Transition
Coaching
Cognitive Behavioural Coaching
Communicator's
Competencies
Creative Manager's
C.R.M.
Cross-cultural Business
Customer Service
Decision-making
Delegation
Developing People
Discipline & Grievance
Diversity*
Emotional Intelligence
Employment Law
Empowerment*
Energy and Well-being
Facilitator's
Feedback
Flexible Working*

Handling Complaints
Handling Resistance
Icebreakers
Impact & Presence
Improving Efficiency
Improving Profitability
Induction
Influencing
Interviewer's
I.T. Trainer's
Key Account Manager's
Leadership
Learner's
Management Models
Manager's
Managing Assessment Centres
Managing Budgets
Managing Cashflow
Managing Change
Managing Customer Service
Managing Difficult Participants
Managing Recruitment
Managing Upwards
Managing Your Appraisal
Marketing
Meetings
Memory
Mentoring

Motivation
Negotiator's
Networking
NLP
Nurturing Innovation
Openers & Closers
People Manager's
Performance Management
Personal Success
Positive Mental Attitude
Presentations
Problem Behaviour
Problem Solving
Project Management
Psychometric Testing
Resolving Conflict
Reward
Sales Excellence
Salesperson's
Self-managed Development
Starting In Management
Storytelling
Strategy
Stress
Succeeding at Interviews
Sustainability
Tackling Difficult Conversations
Talent Management

Teambuilding Activities
Teamworking
Telephone Skills
Telesales
Thinker's
Time Management
Trainer's
Training Evaluation
Training Needs Analysis
Transfer of Learning
Virtual Teams
Vocal Skills
Working Relationships
Workplace Politics
Writing Skills

* only available as an e-book

Pocketfiles

Trainer's Blue Pocketfile of
Ready-to-use Activities

Trainer's Green Pocketfile of
Ready-to-use Activities

Trainer's Red Pocketfile of
Ready-to-use Activities

To order please visit us at **www.pocketbook.co.uk**

09.08.13

ORDER FORM

Your details

Name _____

Position _____

Company _____

Address _____

_____

_____

Telephone _____

Fax _____

E-mail _____

VAT No. (EC companies) _____

Your Order Ref _____

Please send me: | No. copies

The Time Management Pocketbook [ ]

The _____ Pocketbook [ ]

The _____ Pocketbook [ ]

The _____ Pocketbook [ ]

Order by Post
MANAGEMENT POCKETBOOKS LTD
LAUREL HOUSE, STATION APPROACH,
ALRESFORD, HAMPSHIRE SO24 9JH UK
Order by Phone, Fax or Internet
Telephone: +44 (0)1962 735573
Facsimile: +44 (0)1962 733637
E-mail: sales@pocketbook.co.uk
Web: www.pocketbook.co.uk

Customers in USA should contact:
Management Pocketbooks
2427 Bond Street, University Park, IL 60466
Telephone: 866 620 6944   Facsimile: 708 534 7803
E-mail: mp.orders@ware-pak.com
Web: www.managementpocketbooks.com